CW00392700

For Teachers

100 Lines, Sayings, Quotes on Teachers and Teaching

THE GRUMPY GURU

The Grumpy Guru

Copyright © 2018 by The Grumpy Guru

All rights reserved. This book or any portion thereof may not be reproduced or used in any manner whatsoever without the express written permission of the publisher except for the use of brief quotations in a book review.

Printed in the United States of America

First Printing, 2018

ISBN: 9781983105043

http://thegrumpy.guru
http://365ways.me

This book is dedicated to all of you strong people who are taking responsibility of your own feelings and doing something to be better.

All my heartfelt gratitude to the following people: my mom Ruby Jane, you have made me everything I am today; my dad Nestor-- my eternal, my angel, and the source of my perseverance; Mommyling, my spiritual guide ; Ria & Joe, the true witnesses of my transformation and my foundation pillars; Ellie Jane, the sparkle of our eyes;

Juan, thanks for always encouraging me to push harder - you are my ONE; Rocco & Radha, my reason for everything.

The Love of my family and friends is the fountain of inspiration that never runs dry. Thank you for constantly inspiring me, motivating me, and loving me unconditionally.

This book will never be complete without the help of my trusted and talented friends, Roillan James Paña, and everyone at NOW for the moral support.

For reals, I am sick of Chicken Soup! It's not all rainbows and puppies in this world.

I put together a collection of various works to help me find inner strength and peace. I realized that sometimes we just need a real version of ways to feel better and go on with our daily lives.

I am The Grumpy Guru and I know grumpy more than the average grump. I realized that for whatever I am feeling, I had the power to switch to a more positive disposition with a little bit of guidance, a little bit of insight and a line or 2 of text.

I don't think I'll ever stop being grumpy but with the help of these snippets, I can channel them in a positive direction. If this works for me, I can only hope it will work for most people.

This is The Grumpy Guru's take to tackle and manage moments of darkness, doubt, and insecurity.

It's OK to be a grumpy, but Grumps can be Blissfully Happy, too.

I suggest you read what touches you, what helps you move on and what works for you. I've given you 365 different ways and it's up to you what you want to read in this book.

Trust me in my 41 years of grumpiness, I'm still here managing and coping and being relatively happy & content.

Cheers to you guys!

THE GRUMPY GURU

Let's All Be Blissfully Grumpy Together

They are the bridge that connects us to our future. We admire teachers for their tenacity and overwhelming dedication. The willing student sees the value of a great teacher and forget that we follow great men! Teachers are the unsung heroes of this generation. Without expecting too much, they continue to devote their lives to educate and mentor minds that would eventually be responsible for the world.

The Grumpy Guru

\\

Never confine
children to your
way of learning.
They are born in
a different time
with different
perspectives.

//

\\

If kids come to us with healthy minds, it makes our work easier. But if they come to us dysfunctioned, then that makes our work all the more crucial.

//

\\

We want to build
a world where
children chase
after knowledge
and not the other
way around.

//

4

\\

When you're teaching, optimism overflows.

//

5

\\

Our students will only come to see what we value when we value them first.

//

\\

The teacher is the one that nudges you, encourages you and sometimes poke with a stick to press you forward.

//

\\

Teaching is an
art between
preparation
and acting.

//

\\

Teachers build the bridge to help children cross towards their future.

//

\\

Teaching was
never lost.
It's the regard
for it that is.

//

\\

Education is the fire that lists the fuel of knowledge.

//

11

\\

Teaching may not change the world but bringing a small candle that creates a spark.

//

\\

Life is in
education.

//

\\

Teachers are artists that blends the mind and spirit to seek knowledge.

//

\\

Only great
teachers
inspires change.

//

\\

Teaching should
be made simple.
But not simplistic.

//

\\

Education is a
lifetime plan with
the optimism
that better things
are ahead.

//

\\

Teachers are
like candles.
They consume
themselves to give
light to others.

//

\\

The more you
know the more
places you
need to go.

//

\\

Teaching is not
just a profession.
It's an awakener
for every dreamer
from sleep.

//

\\

Only a big heart
can teach little
minds to wander.

//

\\

Teach children to count and count what matters.

//

\\

You are the bow
that is full of
quiver to send
children forth to
their destiny.

//

\\

One can only
appreciate of
teachers that acted
selflessly and
worked tirelessly not
so much on the
material but in
bringing to life
purpose for the
seeking soul.

//

\\

Teaching is the only profession that teaches others to do the same.

//

\\

Teach children
how to think more
than what they
would learn.

//

\\

Learning requires you to act and not just to speculate.

//

\\

After learning something, the next step is to find it.

//

\\

Progress is moving
despite how slow
the movement is.

//

\\

Your mind is
only open to
comprehend if
it's ready for it.

//

\\

Education builds
confidence.

//

\\

Knowing is seeing. Understanding is comprehending and putting it to practice.

//

\\

Teachers should give their students more on something to think about than just homework.

//

\\

The essence of a teacher is more than what they teach in school.

//

\\

It's sad to see people miss so much from learning just because it's opportunity disguised in overalls and call it work.

//

\\

You can only
direct your
students but
never their pace
of learning.

//

\\

Some of the best teachers teach by the heart and not just with a book.

//

\\

If you spoon feed students long enough for them to know the shape but not the function.

//

\\

Never teach
children the way
you were taught
in the past. Unlock
their future and
bring them there.

//

\\

Exhausted
teachers are those
that found no joy
in teaching but
just to keep ahead
of their students.

//

\\

Students should
honor their
teachers for they
teach them the
way of life.

//

\\

You will encounter
two types of
teachers in school:
the one with one
book in hand and
a shotgun in
another and the
other that prods
and teaches you
to fly.

//

\\

Teachers are like walking juggling artists; they need to teach and entertain at the same time.

//

\\

Great teachers teaches more by their perseverance more than their style.

//

\\

A teacher wins the right to teach if only they love to learn themselves.

//

\\

If a teacher wants to do something, they just do.

//

\\

The most
interesting people
you get to meet in
life are those that
point out what you
don't know about
yourself.

//

\\

True teachers are those that learn from the past and find translate it to the present.

//

\\

Teachers either play the part or do the part.

//

\\

As you grow older
you find that
teachers grow
smarter.

//

\\

Teaching is a
wonderful calling
that only a
few actually
understood.

//

\\

Our kids are only
as intelligent as we
help them to be.

//

\\

It's fascinating
how teachers can
be so excited
about the
mundane things.

//

\\

A teachers faith in
her students is in
helping them take
risks and then
help them get to
their destiny.

//

\\

The wonderful
thing about
teaching is that it
doesn't hurt the
teacher and the
one being taught.

//

\\

Learning is a cure to a sad heart. It teaches you how the world works and why it works that way.

//

\\

It belongs to the exceptional few to give students knowledge and wisdom to act upon it.

//

\\

By teaching you
learn.

//

\\

One book to a
child can open up
possibilities.

//

\\

Teachers invite their students to cross over challenges and create their own reality.

//

\\

The only way you can teach is if you had it yourself.

//

\\

Teachers know
that toiling and
perseverance is
part of education.

//

\\

Experience
becomes a great
teacher if it
teaches you.

//

\\

The point of
having to teach a
child is for them to
get along in life
without you.

//

\\

You achieve
immortality by
what you teach
the next
generation.

//

\\

Teachers learn, teach and do at the same time.

//

\\

Encourage the child to learn. Not to be intimidated.

//

\\

Teaching should be something that excited every student to take that next step further.

//

\\

Education is a tool
in which teachers
use to teach a new
way of thinking.

//

\\

A teacher is a fellow traveler who just happened to be ahead of the student.

//

\\

Arouse
enthusiasm and it
will remain in them
for the rest of the
journey.

//

\\

When you give
students
something to do,
they get to think.

//

\\

All that teachers teach are mere references that which students can live for their own.

//

\\

Teaching should be an art that if you do well can even teach to children complex matters that they understand.

//

\\

It is a noble profession and a highly valued gift for teachers to educate students to keep them busy doing good.

//

\\

The best way to teach is to create a way that's simplifies a complex matter enough to turn minds around.

//

\\

To educate is to
toil years of
patience and
compassion.

//

\\

Teachers fan the flames of potential in every student waiting to be lit.

//

\\

It is often a trait of teachers that makes your ears itch until you get the idea.

//

\\

Suggestion is merely a type of teaching to get people curious.

//

\\

Once the child is
taught how to
read the next
thing is to teach
her to believe.

//

\\

A smart person
knows how to
learn and unlearn
as needed.

//

\\

The effectiveness of our teaching is only effective when we have it ourselves.

//

\\

One of the hardest things people must know is that teachers are also humans.

//

\\

Education tells us
how foolish we
truly are.

//

\\

If you don't know something, you must learn from those who do.

//

\\

Teachers are like
the mountains you
stand upon to
look at the valley.

//

\\

Those who are forced to learn a subject knows it best.

//

\\

A teacher loves
three things:
learning, learners
and those two
combined
together.

//

\\

The teacher who is more resolute to teach tolerance is the most intolerant; it ceases the subject to be courageous to question why.

//

\\

It's better to teach one truth than to teach many truths with one lie.

//

\\

Great teachers are like mountains. Mediocre teachers are like staircases; they don't give you much room for hiking.

//

\\

Before you teach a
man to fish, you
must first teach
him to be fair so
he will give more
of himself than he
does taking from
the world.

//

\\

Students often disregard the value teachers bring to their lives. It is only later that they learn and feel grateful for it.

//

\\

Teaching is a profession where you expect nothing but give your everything.

//

\\

Some of the best things you can teach your students is to act more than you talk about it.

//

\\

Measure any
child's
performance
against his past
--not with other
students.

//

\\

Intelligent
ignorance is far
more deadlier
than ignorance
itself for the latter
can be changed
but the former
cannot.

//

\\

Teachers only give students the tools so they can discover better things along the way.

//

\\

Teaching is an art
of stealing; it's a
matter of whom
they steam from
and what to get.

//

\\

Education is a privilege that teachers get to pass on to connect people to the source.

//

Other Titles By
The Grumpy Guru

Strong Women Quotes
Quotes About Changing
Success Quotes
Motivation Quotes
Marriage Quotes
Dog Quotes
Boyfriend Quotes
Happiness Quotes
Inspiring Quotes
What A Life Quotes
Family Quotes
On Love Quotes
Best Friend Quotes
Quotes Friendship
Beach Quotes
Quotes for Life
Encouragement Quotes
Teamwork Quotes

Book Ordering

To order your copy / copies of
Quotes for Teachers:
100 Lines, Sayings, Quotes for Teachers

by The Grumpy Guru,
please visit: thegrumpy.guru.

You can also check out other titles
available.

Bulk Pricing and
Affiliate Programs Available

32962300R00065

Printed in Great Britain
by Amazon